Only the Mountains Do Not Move

A Maasai Story of Culture and Conservation

by Jan Reynolds

Lee & Low Books Inc. • New York

To Noonkuta—for smiling at me, a curious stranger, and welcoming me into her home. And to Ramati—may you blossom into full flower as a proud Maasai woman. —J.R.

A Note About Proverbs
Throughout this book you will read several Maasai proverbs. These short, colorful sayings have been handed down for generations. They are used to give advice or to make a point, and reflect Maasai wisdom, sense of humor, and way of speaking. The proverbs have been translated from Maa, the traditional Maasai language.

LEE & LOW BOOKS Inc., 95 Madison Avenue, New York, NY 10016
leeandlow.com

Manufactured in Singapore by Tien Wah Press, August 2011

Book design by David and Susan Neuhaus/NeuStudio
Book production by The Kids at Our House

The text is set in DelargoDTInfant

HC 10 9 8 7 6 5 4 3 2 1
PB 10 9 8 7 6 5 4 3 2 1
First Edition

Library of Congress Cataloging-in-Publication Data
Reynolds, Jan.
    Only the mountains do not move : a Maasai story of culture and conservation / by Jan Reynolds. — 1st ed.
       p. cm.
    Summary: "A photographic essay about the Maasai people in Kenya, traditionally nomadic herders, exploring the contemporary challenges they face—focusing on environmental changes such as the overgrazing of land and the threat of wildlife extinction—and how the Maasai are adapting their agricultural practices and lifestyle while preserving their culture"—Provided by publisher.
    ISBN 978-1-60060-333-4 (hardcover : alk. paper)   ISBN 978-1-60060-844-5 (pbk. : alk. paper)
1. Maasai (African people)—Kenya—Social life and customs—Juvenile literature. 2. Agriculture—Kenya—Juvenile literature. I. Title.
II. Title: Maasai story of culture and conservation.
DT433.545.M33R48 2011
305.896'5—dc22   2010050879

Nobody can say he is settled anywhere forever; it is only the mountains which do not move from their places. Maasai Proverb

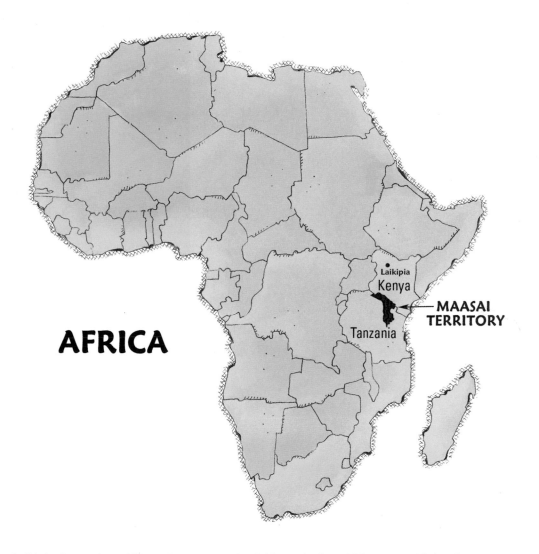

AFRICA

Laikipia
Kenya

MAASAI
TERRITORY

Tanzania

Laikipia, in northern Kenya, is home to the Il Ngwesi tribe of Maasai in this book.

For centuries the Maasai have lived in the heart of East Africa, in an area that covers about 100,000 square miles (161,000 square kilometers) and falls mainly in southern Kenya and northern Tanzania. The people move often, herding their cows and goats and rotating their animals to new grazing land in a balanced rhythm with the wildlife around them. The Maasai today face many changes. The amount of grazing land is shrinking, and the land is becoming dry and barren, threatening their herds and lifestyle. The Maasai are working to adapt to these challenges, while preserving their traditions and environment for generations to come.

Kenya, Africa

Noonkuta, a proud mother, holds a young member of a Maasai tribe—her baby daughter, Ramati. Like other Maasai before her, Ramati will grow up in a close-knit community, learning the ways of her people and respecting the land and animals around her.

Noonkuta and Ramati live in an *enkaji*, a traditional hut with no windows. The enkaji keeps them cool during the day, offering shade from the hot African sun.

The Maasai make enkajis from materials they find in nature. The wooden frame is made from trees lashed together with smaller, more flexible branches. Mud made from the red earth is used to seal the walls. Cow manure is mixed with mud to make an even stronger mud that hardens for the roof.

Women cook inside their huts. The smoke from the cooking fire also helps to keep away bugs.

At night, families sleep on simple wooden beds covered with animal skins. Nets hang over the beds to protect the sleeping people from bugs that bite.

A group of enkajis, arranged in a circle, make up a small village called an *enkang*.

A cow pen sits in the center of the enkang. Dried bushes form a fence to keep the cows in at night.

Livestock are very important to the Maasai. Their entire way of life revolves around taking care of their cows and goats. The animals give them milk and meat, and the animals' skins are made into sandals, furniture, clothing, blankets, and much more. Animals are used in ceremonies and also show how wealthy a family is: the more livestock a family has, the wealthier its members are.

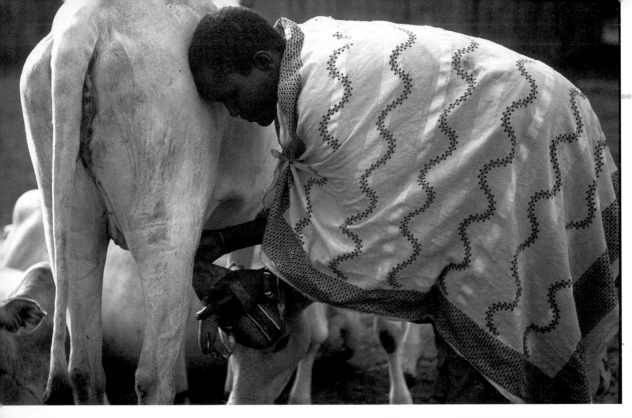

Every morning women milk the cows and goats. The fresh milk will be drunk or made into yogurt.

When the milking is done, the animals are herded out into the bush to graze on wild grasses so they can grow strong and healthy.

Since the animals roam freely while they graze, tribes mark their goats and cows with a line or pattern burned into the hair on an animal's face with a hot stick. Each mark is unique to a specific group of Maasai. The mark allows all Maasai to know which goats and cows belong to each enkang.

One finger does not kill a louse. Maasai Proverb

Outside of the enkang, wild predators such as lions and leopards also roam freely. Men, including Noonkuta's husband, Ole Kiyaa, must work together to keep the herds safe out in the bush.

Women work together too, taking dried gourds down to the river and gathering water for their families. Because the women have to go outside the wall around the enkang, they feel safer walking in a group.

Young people also have jobs to do. Girls collect wood for the cooking fires and tend to the baby goats that are too small to leave the enkang.

Boys learn to tend the cows and goats in the wild. From about the age of fourteen to sixteen, a young man is called a *moran*, which means "warrior." He is part of a close-knit group of other young men who are like brothers. A moran lets his hair grow long and covers it with red earth. As young men reach adulthood—when it is time for the group of moran to become junior elders—they cut their hair.

These young men stay together as a group their entire lives—as children, then as moran, and finally as elders. Although they will have their own individual families, they are bonded as brothers for life, sharing their experiences and supporting one another. Girls are bonded together too, living their lives as sisters even though they will have their own families.

During the hottest part of the day, the goats and the men return to the enkang. The cows stay out grazing, watched by the moran.

Ole Kiyaa looks to see if all of the goats have come back. The Maasai do not count their animals. They know each one by sight. Just by looking, Ole Kiyaa can tell if every animal has returned.

The men then gather to play traditional games such as *bao*, a game of skill in which opponents attempt to capture each other's "seeds," marked by stones on a wooden board.

Ole Kiyaa's young son, Wushon, brings a stool for his father to sit on while he plays. Maasai children respect their elders and appreciate the work they do for the family.

When the children's chores are done, they play games too. These girls play a game similar to jacks. They throw a stone up in the air and try to grab as many other stones as they can from a small hole before the thrown stone hits the ground.

Men and women also thread beads to make bracelets and necklaces, which are worn for decoration.

Much of the day is spent around the enkang in this way, in a peaceful rhythm of activity.

Zebra of course have no huts. Maasai Proverb

The bush outside of the enkang can be dangerous, but the Maasai have a close relationship with the land and wild animals. They respect the power and beauty of the natural environment around them.

Maasai males are very proud of their skills with spears. They learn to throw them with great accuracy when they are very young. The spear is often their only defense against wild animals when they are grazing their livestock. Despite their skills, the Maasai do not hunt wild animals for food. This is looked down upon in their culture.

The Maasai use plants from the natural world in their daily lives. The acacia tree, a common bush plant, has many varieties. One thorny variety is known as a "wait-a-bit." If its thorns catch someone's clothes, the person has to wait a bit to get free.

Roots can also be chewed or boiled into broths to treat digestion and stomach sicknesses.

The Maasai use sticks from one type of acacia as toothbrushes. The tip of a twig is crushed and spread wide, then rubbed against the teeth. The twig is slightly antiseptic, meaning it reduces bacteria and infection; and it keeps people's teeth and gums healthy.

Giraffes also eat thorny acacias. Even though the thorns are sharp, the giraffes' saliva is antiseptic, so cuts on their tongues and in their mouths heal quickly.

The bark of this acacia was stripped off by an elephant that was looking to get moisture from the pulpy wood underneath.

In another, a weaver bird's nests dangle from the branches. The birds build more nests than they need. The extra ones are there to fool predators that might attack young birds in the nests.

Over the years the Maasai have begun to see changes in the land and animals around them. Climate change has caused serious droughts, or water shortages, causing plants and livestock to die. The government has also taken large plots of land to set up wildlife preserves. The Maasai—who do not believe people should own land—now share less space with their herds and the wild animals. Herders are no longer able to rotate their animals to new grazing areas as frequently as before. As a result, the same land is used over and over without time for it to rest and for new plants to grow.

Overgrazing, which occurs when too many plants are eaten by livestock, changes the habitat. The number of plants in the bush is reduced, making it more difficult for wild animals—such as monkeys, giraffes, warthogs, and elephants—to find enough to eat. Without enough to eat, these wild animals are in danger of becoming extinct.

Daylight follows a dark night. Maasai Proverb

Because there is less grazing land, the Maasai herds are shrinking. This affects the way Maasai live, their wealth, and how they feel about themselves. To the Maasai, owning goats and cows means having self-worth.

Faced with these serious changes, many Maasai are finding new ways to live. One of these ways is farming. The Maasai are learning how to plant gardens to grow vegetables.

Streams of water have been created to flow through the fields and irrigate the dry land so that food plants, such as squash, will grow. By farming and adding food plants to their diets, the Maasai have more to eat that does not rely on livestock and grazing. Less grazing means the plant life outside the enkang will be able to restore itself to support more wild animals.

The Maasai are also cultivating wild bees for honey. Homemade bee houses are created with hollowed-out branches and hung in trees.

To attract bees, a man makes a fire and burns dry sansevieria plants. The sansevieria leaves continue to smoke after they are hung in a tree near a bee house. Bees are attracted to the smoking leaves. Within a couple of weeks, the bees make a home in the bee house and fill it with honey.

Some Maasai have even begun working to bring back wild animals that are almost extinct. This powerful black rhino is one of the animals that is in danger of disappearing for good.

People from around the world pay to come and see African wild animals. Guiding visitors through the bush to see the animals in their natural habitat is another new way for the Maasai to make a living. They have built accommodations, such as this big tree house, for visitors to stay in without disturbing the environment or the animals.

The children are the bright moon. Maasai Proverb

Noonkuta and other mothers are comforted to know that the Maasai traditions they learned as children are still being passed on to their own children. But the next generation of Maasai are also learning ways to adapt to a changing environment. They know it is good for everyone to create a balance between the land and the animals, and they are doing just that.

As the sun shines brightly on the mountains, a group of moran comes together. They begin a traditional dance, jumping very high as they sing about the large number of cattle and goats they have and how fat and healthy they are.

While they sing, girls come to listen. The moran ask the girls to join them. Together they dance—a celebration of being Maasai—proud of their herds and their way of life.

Author's Note

In the dark of night, my twelve-year-old son, Briggs, and I slid quietly into the enkaji. As our eyes adjusted, we saw the glowing coals of a fire and an older woman laughing and gesturing as she told her story. Sometimes everyone listening held their breath in suspense, and sometimes they broke out into wild laughter. This was Maasai "school," where the young learned through stories, or oral history. These stories were told most evenings as everyone came together around a smoky fire, and they were told in their native language, Maa. Generation after generation, these stories laced with information and life lessons were passed down, each generation adding to them and embellishing them. Storytelling is one of the ways the Maasai have maintained their culture and lifestyle over time.

For this tribe of Maasai, the Il Ngwesi, it is a challenge to teach their traditional life to their children and to participate in the modern world at the same time. I spent days beside elders who had killed lions in defense of their herds with only knives in their hands. They showed my son and me the scars of the lion's teeth on their bodies to prove it! They had been brave warriors protecting their cattle. But now the biggest challenges for the warriors and youth of the tribe are not coming from the wild. The challenges are coming from the outside world. The Maasai must learn to manage their herds on preserved lands and to deal with problems of overgrazing in limited space.

A new idea follows an old one. Maasai Proverb

People all over the world face similar problems. Natural lands across the United States and in other countries are shrinking as commercial farming, construction, forest cutting, and industrialization spread. The Il Ngwesi elders saw the need for change in their community and are meeting it with environmentally friendly farming and tourism practices. This tribe is a model for adapting to life in the modern world and finding ways to live more sustainably.

Early in the morning after our evening of stories, we drank cow's blood mixed with fresh yogurt, then headed out of the enkang with the animals. While out herding, my Maasai friend tried to explain to me what tourism was like in the wildlife preserve, Maasai Mara. "A leopard sits on the roof of your car," he said. "That's not wildlife in Maasai Mara. It will be gone in a few years. What will happen to their future?"

I thought I understood what he meant. The wildlife was no longer wild in these designated preserves. The natural order was disrupted. And soon, because of this, there would be an imbalance for the animals, land, and people. Still, I wondered what he meant by "What will happen to their future?" Did he mean the future of the animals, the future of the people, or the future of the land? Looking back, I think he meant the future of it all.   —*Jan Reynolds*

GLOSSARY and PRONUNCIATION GUIDE

Some of these words are English adaptations of traditional Maa words. Pronunciations and spellings may vary.

acacia (ah-KAY-sha): thorny tree common to the African wilderness

antiseptic (an-teh-SEP-tik): fighting bacteria, disease, or infection

bao (bow): African strategy game played with stones and a wood board

barren (BAH-ruhn): not able to produce crops or support plant life

bush (bush): unsettled area of wild plants or shrubs

drought (drowt): water shortage caused by lack of rain

enkaji (en-KAH-jee): hutlike Maasai home made of wood and mud, sometimes spelled *inkajijik*

enkang (EN-kahng): group of huts within a circular enclosure

extinct (ek-STINGKT): gone forever; no longer in existence

habitat (HAB-uh-tat): place where a plant or an animal lives

herd (herd): group of animals

Il Ngwesi (eel NUH-gweh-zee): tribe of Maasai from Northern Kenya

irrigate (IHR-uh-gate): to supply water to a field or other area

Laikipia (LIE-kip-ee-ah *or* LIE-keh-pee-ah): district in northern Kenya

lash (lash): to tie together with a rope or chordlike material

livestock (LYVE-stok): domestic or farm animals kept by humans

Maa (mah): native Maasai language

Maasai (MAH-sigh *or* mah-SIGH): semi-nomadic native African people

manure (muh-NOO-ur): dung from cows or other livestock used as fertilizer

moran (MORE-an): young male warrior

Noonkuta (noon-KU-tah): name of Maasai woman

Ole Kiyaa (oh-LEH KEY-ah): name of Maasai man

oral history (OR-ehl HISS-tor-ee): lessons, stories, or customs passed down through spoken word

overgrazing (oh-ver-GRAYZ-ing): overeating of plant life by animals, which causes damage to the environment

predator (PREH-deh-ter): animal that kills and eats other animals

preserve (preh-ZURV): area where land or animals are protected

Ramati (RAH-mah-tee): name of Maasai girl

sansevieria (san-seh-VEER-ee-ah): shrublike plant with long, thin leaves

Washon (WAH-shawn): name of Maasai boy

CHILDREN HELPING CHILDREN

Connect with Maasai children via the Web and find out how you can help build schools for them. Learn from one another while you communicate, and watch schools that your donations help build through photos sent via e-mail. africanconnection.webs.com/

SOURCE NOTES and ACKNOWLEDGMENTS

My main source for this book were the Maasai themselves, specifically the Il Ngwesi of northern Kenya, who welcomed my son and me and allowed us to stay with them, ask questions, and take pictures. I especially wish to thank Noonkuta and her family for sharing their lives, as well as **Gaby Nyausi**, community development officer, educator, and friend.

For vetting information and answering specific questions during the writing process, I offer a special thanks to **J. Terrence "Terry" McCabe**, professor of anthropology for the Environment and Society Program Institute of Behavioral Science at the University of Colorado, Boulder. You are an invaluable resource and a pleasure to know.

The following Web site was also a useful reference during the writing of this book: maasai-association.org/.